I AM JOSEPH

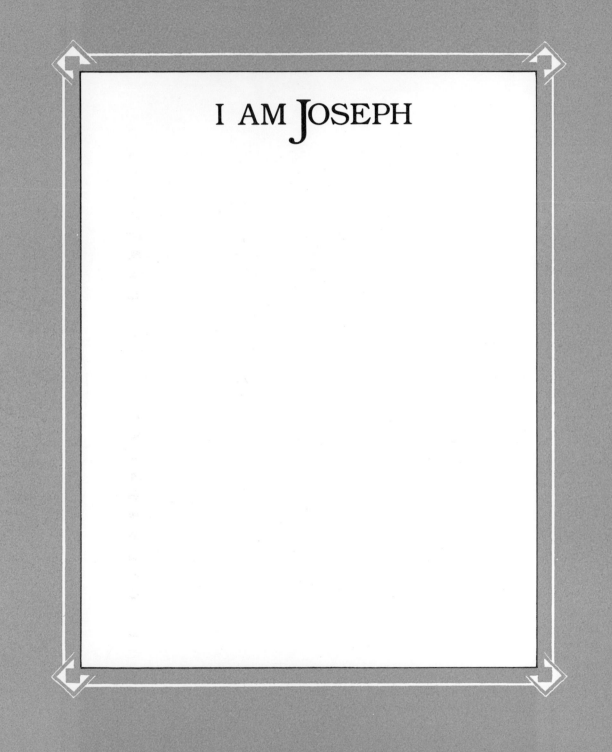

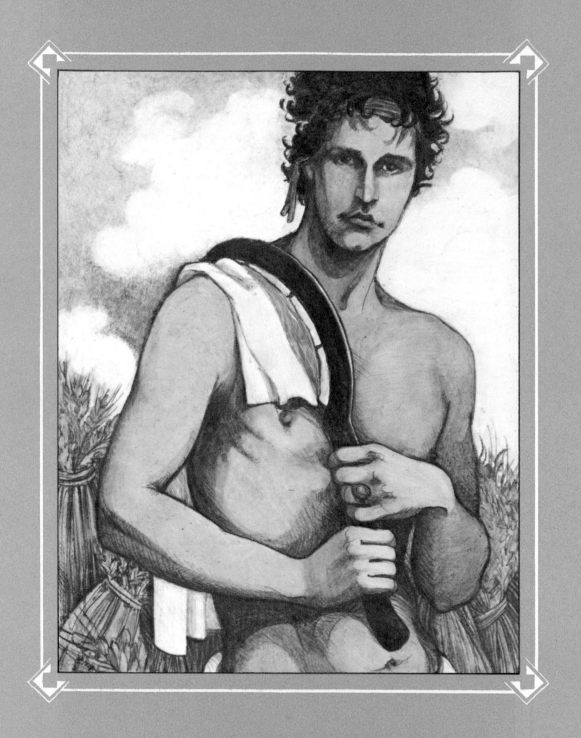

I AM JOSEPH

BARBARA J COHEN

ILLUSTRATED BY CHARLES MIKOLAYCAK

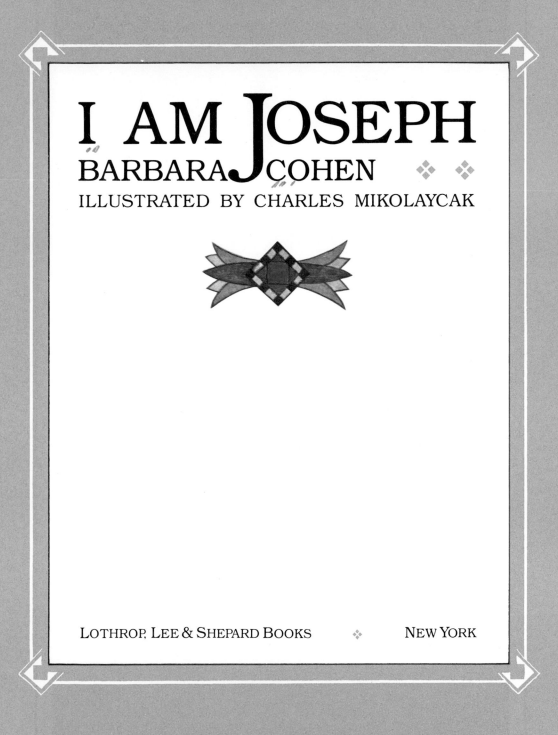

LOTHROP, LEE & SHEPARD BOOKS ❖ NEW YORK

Library of Congress Cataloging in Publication Data
Cohen, Barbara.
I am Joseph.
SUMMARY: Retells the Biblical story of Joseph, from his
viewpoint, relating how he was sold into slavery and became
the Egyptian Pharaoh's adviser.   1. Joseph, the
patriarch—Juvenile literature.   2. Patriarchs
(Bible)—Biography—Juvenile literature.   3. Bible.
O.T.—Biography—Juvenile literature.   [1. Joseph, the
patriarch.   2. Bible stories—O.T.]   I. Mikolaycak,
Charles.   II. Title.
BS580.J6064   222′.11′0924   [B]   79-20001
ISBN 0-688-41933-X   ISBN 0-688-51933-4 lib. bdg.

Book design by Charles Mikolaycak

The author and the artist
dedicate this book
to their editor and friend
Edna Barth

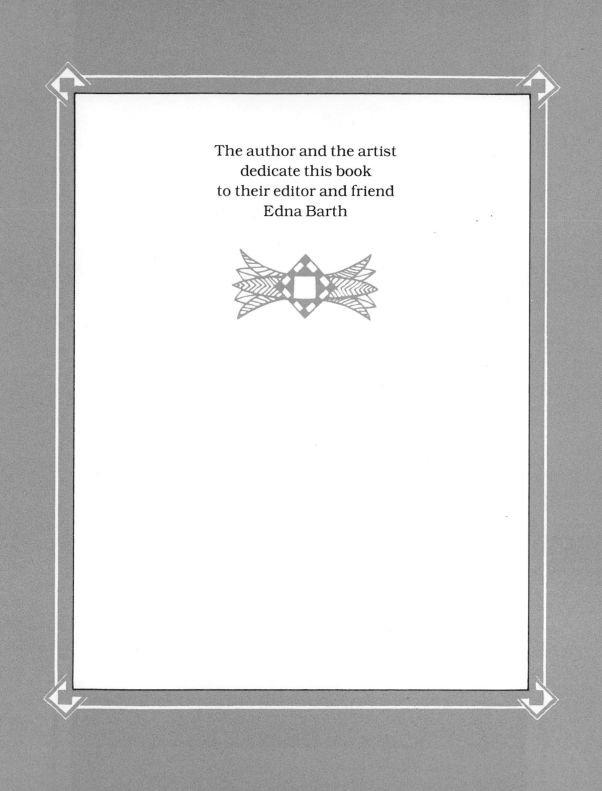

TWELVE BROTHERS

I AM JOSEPH, SON OF JACOB, AND OF RACHEL. ❖WHEN I was seventeen, my father gave me a glorious coat, a coat of many colors. We were twelve brothers, and we were all handsome, but I was the handsomest and I knew it. ❖My mother Rachel was dead. She had been my father's favorite wife and I,

her eldest child, was his favorite son. My father gave me, and only me, the coat of many colors.　❖In those days, I thought my father's love for me was due to my own merit, but later I learned better. I also learned it isn't necessarily a blessing to be the favorite. God tries us all, and in ways we never expect.　❖One winter night, I had a dream. The next day I told the dream to my father and my brothers. "Listen," I said to them, "listen to the dream that I dreamed. We were in a field gathering wheat. We collected the stalks of wheat and bound them together into sheaves. All of a sudden, the sheaf that I'd bound stood upright. And then your sheaves, too, stood upright. Your sheaves all gathered around and bowed down low to my sheaf. That was my dream!"　❖ "What do you think that means?" my brother Judah cried. "Do you think it means you'll rule over us?" And I could see in his eyes that he hated me. I didn't care.　❖ Another night I dreamed another dream, and the next day I told the dream to my father and my brothers. "Listen," I said to them. "Listen to the dream that I dreamed. I was standing in the field and the sun and the moon and eleven stars came, and the sun and the moon and eleven stars all bowed down to me."　❖ This time it wasn't my brother Judah who spoke to me, but my father Jacob himself. "What do you think this dream that you dreamed means? Do you think it means that I and all your brothers, and even your mother, who is dead, will bow down to you?"　❖Little Benjamin was my mother Rachel's only other child. All my brothers except for him looked at me with the hatred I had seen in Judah's eyes. But in my father's eyes I saw questioning and wonder, as if he thought perhaps the truth lived somewhere in my dreams. ❖ That spring my father sent all of his sons except Benjamin and me to Shechem to pasture the flocks. My brothers had been gone for several weeks and we had received no news of them. My father began to worry. I could see it in his face. Finally he called to me, "Joseph!" ❖ "Here I am," I replied. ❖ "Do your brothers feed the flocks in Shechem?" he wondered. "Go now and see if they're well, and if the flocks are well. Bring me back word." ❖ I found my brothers at Dothan. They could see me coming from far away, because of my coat of many colors. No one else had anything like it. They gathered together from all parts of the field and stood close in a group. ❖ When I came near them, they stopped talking. They simply stood there and looked at me in silence. I walked toward them. My skin crawled as I stared at them ranged across my path. But what could I do? There were ten of them and only one of me. Besides, I thought I was safe. I was my father's favorite. ❖ Suddenly they were upon me. Issachar and Zebulun knocked me to the ground. Simeon and Levi took a rope and bound me, while Asher and Gad held my arms and Dan and Naphtali held my legs. Then Simeon and Levi tore my coat from my body, leaving me as naked as the day I was born. ❖ "Let's kill him now," Simeon said. ❖ "We'll throw his body into a pit," Levi agreed, "and tell our father that a wild beast has eaten him up." ❖ "Now," snorted Judah, "we shall see what'll become of his dreams!" ❖ Simeon took his knife from his belt. I saw his hand stretch itself toward my throat. But then Reuben's hand grasped Simeon's by the wrist. "Shed no blood," Reuben ordered. He was the eldest. "Throw him into the pit,

but don't slay him with your own hand." ❖And so they lifted
me up, and carried me to a deep pit, and threw me down into it.
There was no water in it, and I lay bound on the stones at the
bottom. Above me, I could hear them talking. They sat at the

edge of the pit and ate their bread and drank their wine, while I, scratched, bleeding, and naked, suffered hunger, thirst, and pain for the first time in my life. ❖ "Let me out," I cried. "Brothers, brothers, I beg of you, let me out!" But they answered not a word. They went on eating and drinking as if my cries were no more than those of a hawk circling overhead. ❖ After a time, I heard Asher speak in a voice full of excitement. "Look, look, a caravan," he announced. ❖ "Merchants— Ishmaelites or Midianites," Dan explained. "I suppose their camels are carrying spices into Egypt." ❖ "Listen," Judah said. "Listen to me." I knew the others would listen because, though Reuben was the eldest, Judah was the leader. "If we leave our brother here to die, it's the same as if we killed him with our own hands. Let's sell him to the Ishmaelites, so that we're not guilty of murder. For, after all, he is our brother, our own flesh." ❖ "Besides," Asher said, "if we sell him, there's profit in it for us." ❖ They left the pit's edge then, all of them, and they never came back. Instead, two of the merchants scrambled down into the pit and dragged me out of it. Others gave me a coarse loincloth to wrap around my waist and loosened the bonds that bound my legs together. They tied my wrists afresh and told me to walk behind the camels. ❖ And so I did, for seventeen days while we crossed the desert into Egypt, and for ten days more until we came to the great capital city of Thebes. Each noontime they untied my hands so that I could eat. At night they tethered me like a beast to a tree or a bush. During all that journey I could think only of my father. In my mind I could see him staring at my coat of many colors, stained with the blood of some sheep or goat my brothers had killed. I could see him tearing his clothes, putting on sackcloth, and mourning me as he had mourned at my mother's death. And it seemed to me that the evil my brothers had done me was nothing to the evil they'd done my father. Would they know that? He was their father, too.

POTIPHAR

IN THEBES THE EGYPTIANS HELD A GREAT SLAVE MARKET every week. There the merchants sold me to Potiphar, captain of the king's guard. In Egypt the king was called Pharaoh and regarded as a god. Men like Potiphar who were close to Pharaoh were honored like priests. ❖ Because I was a Hebrew, the other servants in Potiphar's house wouldn't sit at the table with me. But I didn't do so badly there. At first I was set to sweeping the floors, whitewashing the walls, and carrying home bundles from the marketplace. I kept my ears open all the time and soon I could speak the language of Egypt as

well as if I'd been born there. ❖ If my master ordered me to bring him a drink of hot liquor, I made sure the drink was very, very hot. And if he ordered me to bring him a drink of luke-warm liquor, I made sure that it was no more than lukewarm.

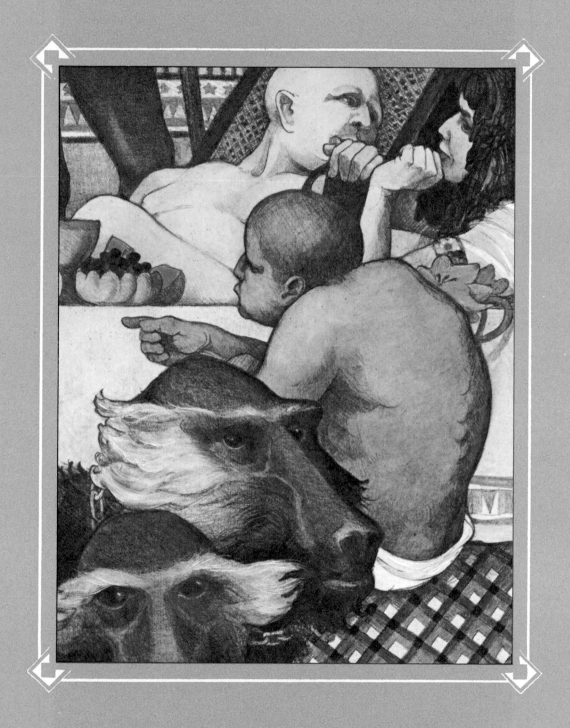

If I was sent to market to trade barley and cotton from my master's farm for oil or wine, I made sure that I got as much wine or oil as I possibly could for as little grain or cotton as I could give up in exchange. ❖ My master noticed me. He gave me garments of fine white cotton to wear, a bronze medallion to hang round my neck, a room of my own to work in, a servant to wait on me, and papyrus scrolls on which to keep his accounts. I took charge of all his business, trading the produce of his farms for the goods brought to Thebes by merchants and traders from east and west, and then selling those goods for gold, silver, and precious gems. My master had been rich when I came to him, but he grew richer and richer. ❖ He was fat and beardless, and his bald head was round and shiny, but I liked him, for he was also shrewd and kind. He had a wife who was much younger than he, and very beautiful. She wore transparent dresses, like a prostitute, and heavy collars of gold around her neck. Sometimes when my master called me to consult with him in his chamber, I saw her there. Other times she and my master entertained guests, and she made me stand behind her couch while I ordered the serving of the meal. She did this because I was good-looking and she wanted to show me off, especially if members of the nobility were dining with them that day. She would rise to compliment me on the way the meal had been served. She would stand very close to me as she spoke, and smile at me. Her nearly naked body would brush against mine, and I could smell her musky perfume. I was young, after all, and in the fullness of my powers, but my master had been good to me. I would not let my face show my feelings. ❖One morning, while I was working at the accounts, she came into my room unannounced. She sent my servant away, and then she took my hand. "Lie with me, Joseph," she said. ❖I longed to do as she asked, but I wouldn't. "Mistress," I said, "my master doesn't even know what's in his house. He's put it all into my hands. The only thing he hasn't put into my hands is you, his wife. How can I do what you ask of me, and in that way sin not only against my master, but against God Himself?" She couldn't understand about God for she worshiped the cat and the crocodile, but I thought she could understand about her husband. ❖She was angry with me. I could see it in her face. Without saying another word, she left my room. I was glad because if she persisted, there was no way the matter could end well for me. I prayed that she'd forget about me. ❖ But she didn't. I was there in the household all the time, and her passion grew greater every day. Each morning she came to me after Potiphar had left the house and made the same request of me. And each day I answered her as I had answered her on the first day. ❖ Then, on one particular morning, the house was silent. It was the day of a great festival in honor of the river Nile, and even the lowest slave had been given a holiday. As a Hebrew, who worshiped only one God, the God of my fathers, I didn't go out. I was sure I was in the house all by myself. I sat in my room, casting up my master's accounts, when suddenly, without warning, my mistress appeared before me. I rose when I saw her and bowed low. ❖ "Don't bow before me, Joseph," she said. ❖I straightened up. She reached out her hand and grasped the knot by which

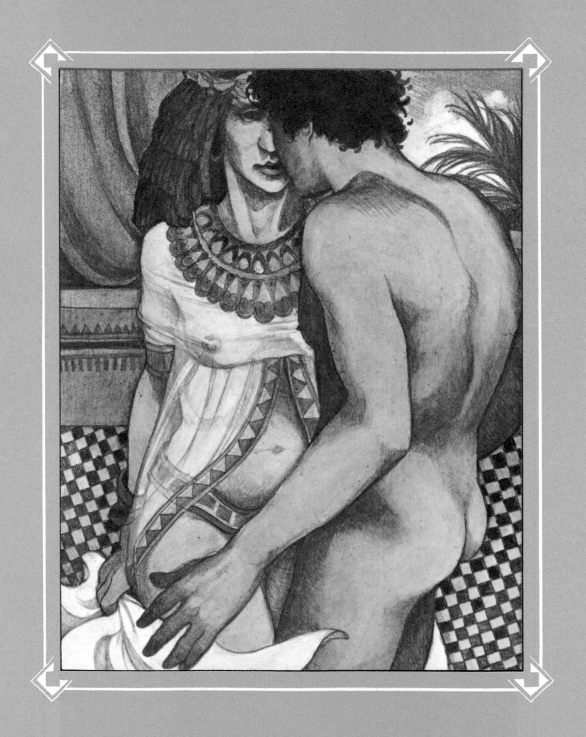

my loincloth was held in place. "Lie with me, Joseph," she said yet again. She pulled at the knot, it came undone, and my loincloth was in her hand. Her eyes grew wide as she beheld my nakedness, but I, not sure of the strength of my own will, turned as quickly as I could and fled away from her. I left her there, standing in my room with my garment in her hand.

Later, when I returned, she was gone, and so was my loin-cloth. ❖ And then I was afraid. But where was I to go? My appearance was such that I would have been recognized any-where if the alarm was set for me. There wasn't an Egyptian living who was tall and fair like me. ❖ So I stayed where I was. In the middle of that very night, my master came into my room with his wife and two soldiers from Pharaoh's guard. "You came to mock me," cried my master's wife. She spit the words at me in fury. "Did you think I wouldn't tell my husband what the Hebrew slave he brought into my house did to me? You came to me on my couch, and you took off your garment, and when I cried out, you ran away, leaving it behind." She held out her hand and in it I could see she held my loincloth, rolled up into a ball. "Even so," she went on, "even so, I told my husband as he held me in his arms, even so did your servant Joseph try to do to me." ❖ The guards seized me and tied me up. All the while she shouted and screamed at me. But my master only looked at me with sad eyes and said noth-ing. ❖ The soldiers carried me off to prison. It was the prison where the king's prisoners were bound, and I was kept for three long, dark, and weary years in that prison. ❖ But even there I managed to make my way. When the prison keeper went out, I would wash the cups, make the beds, and lay the tables. And so the prison keeper, like Potiphar before him, put me in charge of all the labor that went on in the prison and made my life as comfortable as he dared. He did no work as long as I was there. ❖ Soon after I'd taken charge of the prison, Pharaoh found a fly in his cup of wine and a pebble in the cake he was eating. What worse crime could a butler commit than to fail to serve the wine as it should be served? What worse crime could a baker commit than to fail to bake a cake as it should be baked? So Pharaoh had both his chief butler and his chief baker thrown into prison, into the same prison in which I lived. For a year we continued together in that prison. We became friends, after a fashion. ❖ One morning, when I came into the cell in which they lived, I saw that the butler and the baker were both troubled. No day in prison was full of joy, but life went on there, as it does anywhere, and some days were better than others. I knew no reason why this day should be a bad one, so I said to my two companions, "Why do you look so worried today?" ❖ The butler answered, "Each of us dreamed a dream last night, and no one can tell us what our dreams mean." ❖ "God knows what your dreams mean," I replied. "Let me hear them. Perhaps God will reveal their meaning to me." ❖ They knew I was a clever man, though only a Hebrew slave, and so they told me their dreams. "In my dream," the butler said, "I saw a vine before me. The vine had three branches. As it was budding, its blossoms shot forth, and then immediately the clusters of blossoms brought forth ripe grapes. In my dream I was holding Pharaoh's cup. I took the grapes and pressed them into the cup, and then I gave the cup right into Pharaoh's hand!" ❖ "Listen," I said. "The three branches are three days. In three days Pharaoh will forgive you. You'll give Pharaoh's cup directly into his hand, just as you used to do." ❖ Of course, the butler was pleased with my explanation of his dream. "I hope you're telling me the truth,"

he said. ❖ "You'll know soon enough," I answered. "Remember me when all's well with you. Mention me to Pharaoh and bring me out of this prison. I was stolen away out of my country. I committed no crime there, and none here, that I should be walled up in a dungeon." ❖ The butler promised that he wouldn't forget me. And then the baker told me his dream. "I was carrying three baskets of white bread on my head. In the top basket were all kinds of baked delicacies for Pharaoh. Then some birds came and ate up all the food in the baskets. Why did they do that? I don't understand any of it." ❖ "Listen," I said. "The three baskets are three days. In

three days Pharaoh will remember you. He'll have you hung from a tree, and the birds will eat your flesh from off your bones." ❖ The baker's jaw dropped so low it looked as if it would touch his belly. "Perhaps what you say isn't true," he suggested. ❖ "Perhaps you're right," I said. ❖ But the third day after that was Pharaoh's birthday. He made a feast for all his servants. He remembered the chief butler and the chief baker. I suppose he thought, "A fly can put itself into a drink when no one's looking, but if a pebble falls into a cake, it isn't by accident." So he restored the chief butler to his butlership, but he hanged the baker, as I had said he would. ❖ Yet the chief butler didn't remember me. I had to live in the darkness of that prison for two more years.

PHARAOH

THERE WERE TIMES IN PRISON WHEN I GAVE UP HOPE. I thought that I'd never be freed, that I'd die in that terrible place, and never see the sun's light again. But then I remembered those who had gone before me, my great grandfather Abraham and my great grandmother Sarah. Who would have thought that my grandfather Isaac would be born to them in their old age? I remembered my father Jacob. Who would have imagined that he, who crossed the river Jordan possessing nothing but his staff, should grow to be the richest man in all the land of Canaan? God didn't desert Abraham, Isaac, or Jacob, and he wouldn't desert me, for had I not dreamed that I would be as powerful as a king? ❖ And so it happened. After two years, Pharaoh sent to the prison for me. Guards came and got me and brought me to the palace. There, I bathed myself, and curled my hair, and shaved my beard, which had grown long and thick while I was in prison. Before, I'd been a boy, but now I was fully a man. Then I rubbed my body with oil and perfume and dressed myself in clean white cotton that a serving maid brought for me. ❖ "Lovely maiden," I said, "kind servant of the great king, do you know why I'm here?" I smiled at her. "Do you know why a Hebrew slave was suddenly pulled out of prison and brought to the palace of the supreme and sacred ruler?" ❖ "Is it possible," she asked softly, "that you can tell the meaning of dreams?" ❖ "Yes," I said. "Sometimes God enables me to do that." ❖ "And would anyone in Pharaoh's household know that?" she asked once more. ❖ "Yes," I said. "Pharaoh's chief butler would know that, though I was sure he'd forgotten me long ago." ❖ She straightened a fold in the pleated loincloth she'd helped me put on. "Last night," she said, "the god king had dreams. They disturbed his rest, and in the morning he called in all his priests and magicians to tell him what they meant. But it seems that none of their answers satisfied him. He's been sending all over the city for anyone who's ever been known to tell the

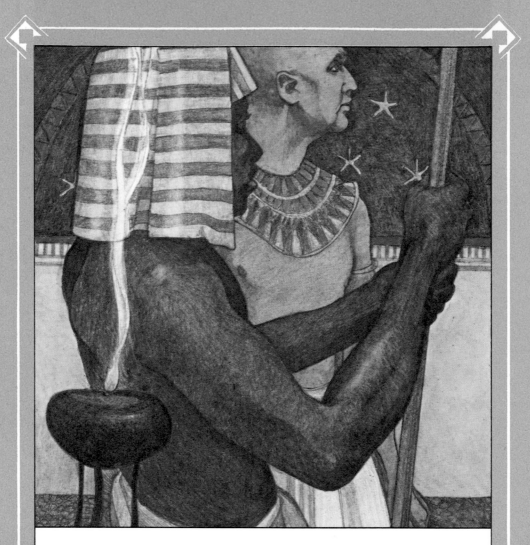

meaning of a dream. It appears that one of those people is you!" ❖ Then other soldiers came and got me. They led me into the great throne room. It was so huge five hundred men could attend Pharaoh and still not fill it up. The mighty king

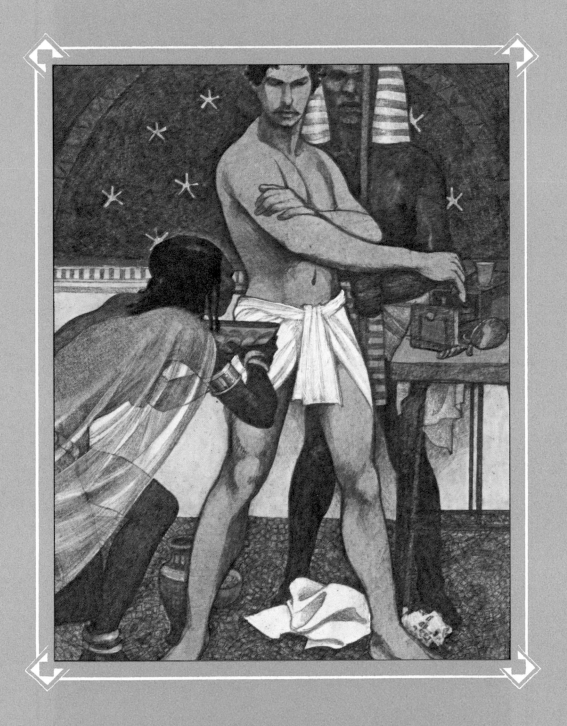

sat on a carved stone chair. Two carved stone lions crouched on either side of him. As was the custom, I threw myself down flat on my face before him. ❖ "Lift yourself up," Pharaoh said, "and listen to me." ❖ I stood before Pharaoh and looked at him. His face was unsmiling and severe, but there was no mindless cruelty in his eyes. ❖ "I've dreamed dreams," Pharaoh said. "I sent for all my wise men and all my magicians, and not one has been able to tell me what my dreams mean. My butler remembered that when you hear a dream you can interpret it." ❖ "The meaning of dreams doesn't come from me," I replied. "It's God who'll give Pharaoh an answer of peace." ❖ "Let it be from your god or from you, so long as I understand," Pharaoh said. "In my dream, I stood upon the brink of the river. Seven fine-looking fat cows came up out of the river and fed on the reeds growing along the bank. And then seven other cows came up after them, and these were poor, ugly, thin cows. In all of Egypt I never saw such miserable cattle. All of a sudden, the thin cows ate up the fat cows. But you'd never have known it to look at them, because they were just as scrawny after their meal as they'd been before. Then I woke up." Pharaoh paused and looked at me. ❖ "But there was more," I said. ❖ He nodded. "Yes," he said. "There was more. I slept again, and I dreamed again. Seven ears of barley grew on one stalk, and they were good, full ears. Seven withered ears, thin and blasted by the east wind, grew up behind the good ears. And the withered ears swallowed up the good ears." He shook his head, frowning. "I awoke, and told my dreams to my magicians, but none of them could find any sensible meanings in either of my dreams." ❖ "The two dreams are one, mighty Pharaoh," I explained. "God has told Pharaoh what He's about to do. The seven fat cows are seven fat years, and the seven good ears are the same seven years; the dreams are one. And the seven thin cows that came up after them are seven more years, and the seven empty ears blasted by the east wind, they're the same seven years; they're seven years of famine. God has blessed Pharaoh with a warning of what's to come. There will be seven years of great plenty throughout Egypt. After that, there will be seven years of famine; all the plenty will be forgotten. Famine will eat up the land, and abundance will be unknown. It'll be forgotten, so great will be the famine. That's why the dream was doubled—to warn Pharaoh of the greatness of the famine. This thing has been ordained by God. It will happen soon." ❖ Once more I fell on my face before Pharaoh, but this time I got up again of my own accord. Pharaoh stared at me for a long time before he spoke. Then he asked quietly, "What should I do about this?" ❖ "Let Pharaoh find a man," I said. "Let him find a wise and careful man and set him up over the whole land of Egypt. This man will send out overseers who'll collect a fifth part of the harvest during the years of plenty and store it in the cities. If this is done, when the famine comes, the land of Egypt will not die." ❖ Pharaoh turned to the advisers, priests, wise men, and magicians who stood about him. "Can we find such a man?" he asked them. "Can we find a man in whom understanding and knowledge live?" Immediately he turned back to me. "Because your god has shown you all of this, there's no one

so full of knowledge and understanding as you. You're to be in charge of all my house. All my people will be ruled by what you say. Only I will be greater than you." He beckoned me forward. I approached the throne. "Hold out your right hand,"

he said. He took off a signet ring from his own finger and put
it on mine. "See," he announced to all who were present, "I
have set Joseph over all the land of Egypt." Then he ordered
me dressed in a linen robe woven with gold thread, and with

his own hands he hung a golden chain around my neck. ❖ He sent me forth into the city in a jewel-encrusted chariot. Heralds went before me shouting, "Let all bend their knee before the wisest man of Pharaoh. Let all bend their knee before Zaphenath-paneah." That was my new name, the Egyptian name that Pharaoh gave me, and it means "He who reveals that which is hidden." ❖ Pharaoh gave me a wife, too. Her name was Asenath, and she was the daughter of the priest of On. She was a hundred times better to look upon, and a thousand times better to know, than ever was Potiphar's wife. She came to me willingly, though I was a Hebrew and would never sacrifice to her gods. She bore me two sons. I called the second one Ephraim, from the Hebrew word meaning "to be fruitful," because God had made me fruitful even in the land of my suffering. And I called the eldest Manasseh, from a word that means "making to forget," because it seemed that I'd forgotten all my sorrow, all my pain, and all who lived in my father's house. But I hadn't forgotten. I hadn't forgotten anything. ❖ For seven years of plenty I traveled up and down the land of Egypt. The earth brought forth heaps and heaps of food, and I had it gathered up and stored in all the cities. I laid by so much grain that we left off counting it; it was no more to be counted than the sands of the sea. ❖ The seven years of plenty came to an end, and the seven lean years began. There was famine in all the lands around Egypt, but in Egypt there was bread. I opened the storehouses, and sold the Egyptians grain. People from other countries came to me to buy grain, too, because hunger was everywhere.

DREAMS COME TRUE

PHARAOH HAD ORDERED A LUXURIOUS PALACE BUILT FOR me. In the courtyard, I received delegations from foreign countries who came to buy from Egypt's stores. ❖ And one day they came to my house, the ones I had been waiting for. They came, my ten brothers, the same ten who had thrown me into a pit and sold me to the Ishmaelites. They came, and I knew them, but they didn't know me. They'd been men when I'd last seen them, and I'd been only a boy. Besides, I was now called by another name. ❖ In the courtyard they bowed down to me, their faces hidden in the earth. I made up my mind not to speak directly to them, but to use a translator, as if I didn't know their language. I said to them, "Where do you come from?" ❖ Reuben, who was the eldest, lifted his head to reply. "From the land of Canaan, to buy food." ❖ "You're spies," I accused. "You've come to spy out the land, to see where you might launch an attack to seize all our food stores for yourselves." ❖ Judah jumped to his feet. "No, no, my lord," he cried. "We're your servants. We've come only to buy food. We're all one man's sons; we're all honest men. Your servants are no spies." ❖ "Not so," I repeated. "You've come to spy out the land." ❖ "We're your servants," Judah

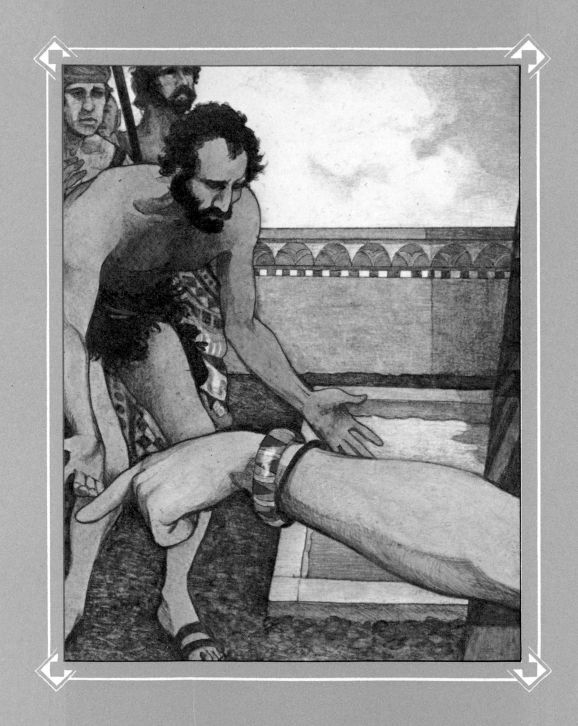

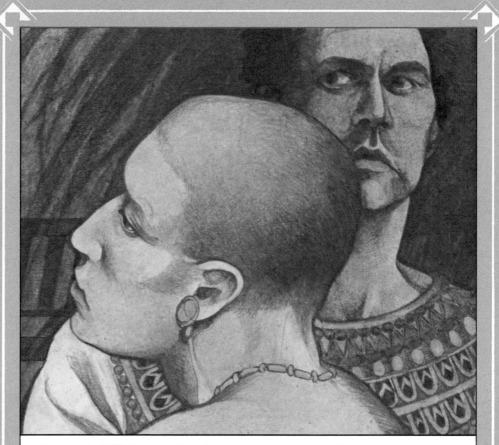

insisted. "We're twelve brothers, the sons of one man in the land of Canaan. Our youngest brother isn't with us. He stayed behind with our father." ❖ "That makes eleven," I said, "not twelve." ❖ Judah's eyes fell to the ground. "The twelfth is gone," he answered quietly. ❖ "Probably back to your country," I said, pretending anger, "to report the information you've gathered. Now I'll prove whether or not you speak the truth. As Pharaoh lives, you won't leave unless your youngest brother comes here. Send one of your number to fetch your brother. He won't risk his life to come if he's not your brother, and so I'll know if you're honest men or spies." ❖ I kept them in my house under close guard for three days so they would know I wasn't to be trifled with. But I also saw to it that they had plenty to eat and drink. Then on the third day I came to them and said, "Do as I say and you'll live. I fear God; I'm a man of my word." ❖ They bowed low to me, and once again their faces touched the ground. ❖ "If you're honest men, let one of you remain here, bound and under guard, as a hostage," I went on. "The rest of you go, and carry grain to your houses to ease the famine, and bring your youngest brother back to me. If he comes, I'll know you speak the truth. If you speak the truth, you won't die." ❖ They began to talk to each other in their own language, never imagining that I could understand what they were saying. Judah sighed. "We're guilty men," he said. "God has not forgotten our brother Joseph, who begged us to set him free, and we wouldn't listen to him. That's why we're in this trouble now." ❖ "Don't you remember," Reuben scolded, "don't you remember when I told you not to sin against the boy? You wouldn't listen. We didn't actually kill him with our own hands, but God requires our punishment because it's as though we did slay him." ❖ As I listened to the words of Judah and Reuben, I could barely control myself. I turned away from them, and went out of the room and wept. But I had lived as a slave and wasted away in prison for a long time. I was not ready to reveal myself. ❖ When I'd shed all my tears, I washed my face and came back to them. "This is the one," I said. "This is the one I choose to be my hostage." And I pointed to Simeon, bloodthirsty Simeon. My guards came and bound him while the others watched, their faces white with fear. Then I told my servants to fill my brothers' sacks with grain, and to put the money they'd brought with them to pay for the grain back into their sacks, and to give them extra food to eat along the way. My instructions were carried out, my brothers' donkeys were loaded with grain, and they set out, leaving Simeon behind. ❖I had thought to see them again in a few weeks. Yet a whole year passed and they hadn't returned. While Simeon was my hostage, I ordered him well-treated, but I didn't go to see him. I didn't trust myself. ❖And one day, after more than a year had passed, I looked out of a window of my house and there in my courtyard I saw my brothers. Nine had gone away from me; ten had returned. Benjamin was with them. I called my steward and said to him, "Go out and bring those men you see out there into the house. Butcher some cattle and prepare the meat. I want those men to dine with me at noon." ❖My steward went into the courtyard to speak with them. I listened and watched from the window. When my steward told them to come in to dine with me, Levi frowned and wrinkled his dark brow. "He's going to make slaves out of us," Levi said in our native tongue. "That's why he's bringing us into his house—to accuse us and make slaves of us. He put the money we gave him last time back into our sacks so that when he had the chance, he could claim we stole it, and then seize our pack animals, and us, in return for it!" ❖Judah approached my steward, and through the translator he

said, "Last time we left here, we found that the money we'd used to pay for the food had been put back into our sacks." Judah reached into the leather bag he carried at his waist and took out a pile of coins. He pressed them into my steward's hand, saying, "Here's the money back again, and more money besides to buy food. We don't know who put it into our sacks." ❖ But my steward returned the money to him. "Peace, peace, good man," he said. "Luck, chance, or your god put

treasure in your sacks; I had your money." After that, he had Simeon brought to them. He fed their animals and then he brought my brothers into my house to wash. ❖When I came to meet them in the great hall, they bowed low and presented me with gifts—salves, honey, spices, opium, nuts, and almonds. They said their father had sent me all these precious things. "Is your father well?" I asked. "Is that old man of whom you spoke still alive?" ❖"Your servant, our father, is well," Reuben said. "He's still alive." ❖Then I looked at Benjamin, my mother's son, and saw that he was tall and straight, with curling black hair and eyes as green as my mother's had been. I pointed to him and said, "Is this your youngest brother, the one you told me about?" ❖ "Yes," Reuben replied. "He's our youngest brother, the apple of our father's eye, the darling of his heart." ❖"My lord, I left my own sons as guarantee of his safety," Judah said. "If I hadn't done that, our father wouldn't have let him come. But we knew we didn't dare come back to you without him." ❖Benjamin smiled, and his smile was as sweet as the honey he'd carried with him from the land of Canaan. The others were in awe of me, but not he. "My father feared I'd be lost to him if I went away, as were Joseph and Simeon before me," Benjamin said, as easily as if he were the eldest and not the youngest. "But Judah told our father that I would surely die and all the rest of us, too, if we didn't get our hands on something to eat." ❖When I heard the voice of my brother, my mother's child, I said to him, "God be gracious to you, my son." As I had done once before, I hurried out of the room and went to my own chamber, and there I wept.

Afterward, I washed my face and came back to them. ❖ It was time to eat. I sat at a table by myself, members of my household sat at another table, and my brothers sat at yet a third. I instructed my servants to feed all my brothers generously, but to give to Benjamin five times as much as they gave to the others. We all ate and drank and laughed together, and none of my brothers complained that Benjamin got more than they, or even seemed to notice it at all. ❖When the meal was over, I called my steward to my side and commanded him in a voice no one else could hear. "Fill the men's sacks with food, as much as they can carry," I said. "Put each man's money back in his sack once more. And then take my precious silver cup, and put it in the sack that the youngest one carries, along with his grain and his money." ❖My steward did as I instructed. With the first light of morning, my brothers and their caravan of animals were on their way. When time enough had passed for them to be well out of the city, I said to my steward, "Follow those men. When you overtake them, say to them, 'Why have you traded evil for good? You've taken my lord's cup; you've done an evil thing.'" ❖If my steward was surprised at my instructions, he gave no sign. He knew that the cup had been placed in Benjamin's sack by my order, but he was accustomed to doing as he was told without question. And so, with some other servants, he rode out. Half a day later, he returned. All eleven of my brothers were with him. Their faces were troubled, but their shoulders were straight and their heads were high as my servants escorted them into my presence. ❖They fell to the ground before me, and I said to them,

"What is this thing you've done? How foolish to do this thing to
a man such as I!"   ❖ Judah lifted his head to answer me. "My
lord, what can we say? How can we clear ourselves? You won't
believe what we say, and why should you? And anyway, it
doesn't matter. God is punishing us for another evil, one that
we really did commit. We're all of us your slaves now—the one
in whose sack the cup was found and all the rest of us, too."
❖ I held up my hand. "Oh, no," I said. "It would be a sin on

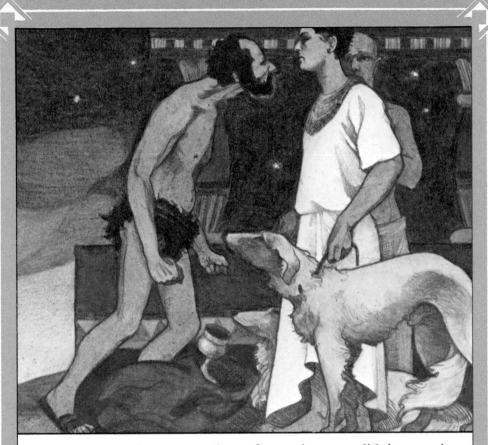

my part to make you my slaves for a crime you didn't commit. Only the man in whose sack the goblet was found will be my slave. As for the rest of you, go back to your father. Go back to your father in peace." ❖ Judah rose to his feet. His hands clenched so tightly into fists that I could see his knuckles turn white. He came close to me, as close as he dared, and he spoke to me in a voice so low the others couldn't hear him. "If we go home to our father and the boy Benjamin isn't with us, our father will die. His soul is bound up with the soul of the boy, and he'll die at the very thought of never seeing him again. I beg you, let me stay with you as your slave instead, and let the boy go back with his brothers. How can I look at my father if the boy isn't with me? How can I watch my father die?" ❖ Judah, Judah, I dreamed so many dreams, but did I ever dream that I would hear you speak such words? ❖ Now was the moment. I could wait no longer. I sent my servants away. I sent the translator away. I wept, and this time I didn't trouble to hide my tears. I stood before my brothers and in my mother tongue I cried out to them, "I am Joseph, I am Joseph. Does my father live? Does he truly live?" ❖ My brothers were frightened. They scrambled to their feet and backed away from me as if I were a ghost. I spoke to them softly, so as to calm them. "Come close to me," I said. "I beg you, come close to me." ❖ Slowly they approached me. "I am Joseph," I repeated. "I am Joseph, your brother, whom you sold into Egypt. Don't be grieved with yourselves anymore for selling me. God sent me here ahead of you to save lives. There's been famine for two years, and there are five more years of famine to come. God sent me before you, to save you alive." ❖ My brothers fell to the ground before me once again, but I went to each one of them and raised him up with my own hands. "It wasn't you who sent me here," I explained. "It was God. God has made me a friend to Pharaoh, and lord of his house, and ruler over all the land of Egypt. Get up and go to my father, and tell him to come down into Egypt. Don't wait. Tell him he'll live in the land of Goshen. He'll be near me, he and you, your wives and your children, your flocks and your herds—all that you have." ❖ My brothers rose to their feet and looked at me. ❖ "Your eyes see," I told them, "and the eyes of my brother Benjamin see. It is I, Joseph, who speaks to you. Tell my father of all my glory in Egypt. Tell him of all that you've seen. Hurry and bring my father here." ❖ I went over to my brother Benjamin. I embraced him and I wept. My brother Benjamin wept, too. ❖ Then I embraced Reuben, Judah, Issachar, Zebulun, Dan, Naphtali, Gad and Asher. I even embraced Simeon and Levi. And they embraced me. And we wept; all of us wept. Then we talked until long after darkness fell and I had to send for the lamps. ❖ When Pharaoh heard that my brothers had come, he sent wagons full of food for them. To each he gave a fine woven robe, but to Benjamin he gave five, and three hundred shekels of silver besides. To my father, Pharaoh sent ten donkeys carrying barley and bread and all the other good things of Egypt for him to eat on his way. I sent my brothers home with all those wagons and animals laden with goods, and I said to them, "Don't quarrel on the road." ❖ They laughed, as if such a thing couldn't happen among us again. ❖ And so, two months later, Jacob came to Egypt. He came with his sons, their wives, and their children. He came with the wagons that Pharaoh had sent him, and all his flocks, and all his goods. So great was his caravan that it stretched as far as the eye could see. ❖ I, Joseph, went out to meet him. In the midst of the land of Goshen, my father and my brothers bowed down to me. I held up my hand to them. "Don't bow before me, your son, your brother," I said. "My

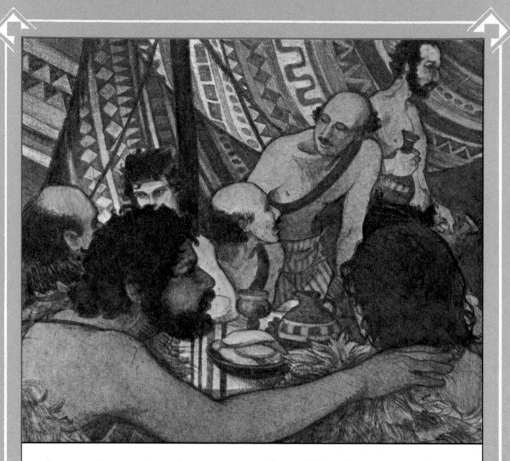

dreams have already come true." ❖ We all embraced one another. And then we went into a great tent pitched in the middle of the field, and we feasted together, all of us, seated at the same table. ❖ My father Jacob lived in Egypt until the day that he died. My brothers, Reuben, Simeon, Levi, Judah, Issachar, Zebulun, Dan, Naphtali, Gad, Asher, and Benjamin, and I, too, I Joseph, we live there still. Here we will remain for so long as God wills. And when He wills that we go, we will go.

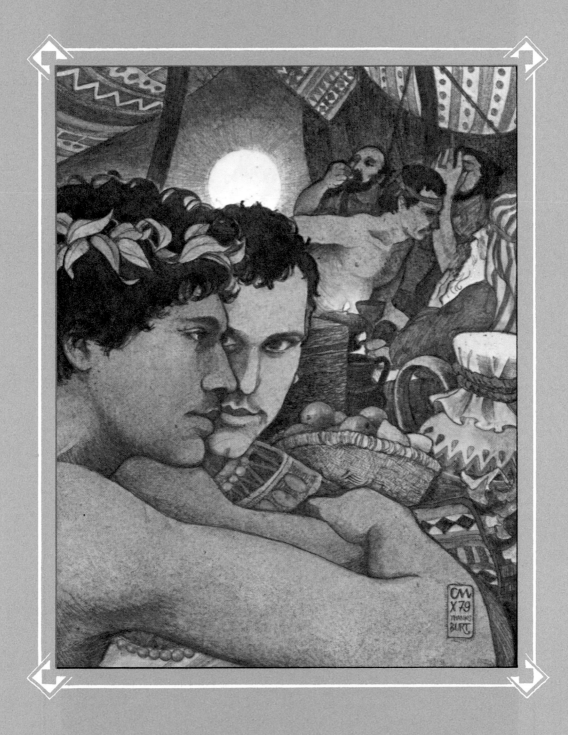

BARBARA COHEN, a former English teacher, is a newspaper columnist, novelist, and storyteller. She is perhaps best known for *The Carp in the Bathtub,* a story that has been hailed as a "little classic." She is also highly regarded for her novels, which include *Thank You, Jackie Robinson, Bitter Herbs and Honey,* and *The Innkeeper's Daughter.* Her first Bible story for young readers was *The Binding of Isaac,* illustrated with paintings by Charles Mikolaycak.

CHARLES MIKOLAYCAK, a distinguished graphic designer and illustrator, has received many honors for his children's books. He is especially noted and commended for his careful research to provide authentic detail in his paintings. The pictures for *I Am Joseph* were done in the same size as printed in the book, using colored pencils with oil glazes.